INSTANT-FLEX 718

Also by Heather Phillipson

Faber New Poets 3 (Faber and Faber, 2009)

NOT AN ESSAY (Penned in the Margins, 2012)

HEATHER PHILLIPSON

INSTANT-fLEX 718

718

BLOODAXE BOOKS

Copyright © Heather Phillipson 2013

ISBN: 978 1 85224 970 0

First published 2013 by
Bloodaxe Books Ltd,
Highgreen,
Tarset,
Northumberland NE48 1RP.

www.bloodaxebooks.com
For further information about Bloodaxe titles
please visit our website or write to
the above address for a catalogue.

Supported by
**ARTS COUNCIL
ENGLAND**

Cover design by Ed Atkins and Heather Phillipson

Printed in Great Britain by
Bell & Bain Limited, Glasgow, Scotland.

ACKNOWLEDGEMENTS

Thanks are due to the following publications in which some of these poems first appeared: *AnOther, Ambit, Bloomberg New Contemporaries exhibition catalogue 2011, City State: New London Poetry* (Penned in the Margins, 2009), *Dear World & Everyone in It: New Poetry in the UK* (Bloodaxe Books, 2013), *English Chicago Review, Fin, Five Dials* (Hamish Hamilton), *Fuselit, Heather Phillipson: Faber New Poets 3* (Faber and Faber, 2009), *Jubilee Lines* (Faber and Faber, 2012), *London: a History in Verse* (Harvard University Press, 2012), *Lung Jazz: Young British Poets for Oxfam* (Cinnamon Press, 2012), *Magma, Manhattan Review, Missing Slate, nthposition, Pen Pusher, Poetry London, The Rialto, Rising, The Shuffle Anthology, Southbank Poetry, The Spectator, Stop Sharpening Your Knives vols. 3, 4 & 5* (Eggbox 2009/2010/2013), *The Troubadour Poetry Prize, Versuch*, and *Voice Recognition: 21 Poets for the 21st Century* (Bloodaxe Books, 2009).

'The Horsey Mail' and 'The Horse Jacuzzi' were commissioned by the British Film Institute. '1960s Monochrome Hollywood Paraphernalia ($47, collection only)' was commissioned for the Psycho Poetica project, curated by Simon Barraclough. 'Relational Epistemology' and '1960s Monochrome Hollywood Paraphernalia ($47,collection only)' were first broadcast on BBC Radio 3's *The Verb*; 'Le Parc' was first broadcast on BBC2 television.

Thanks to The Society of Authors for an Eric Gregory Award in 2008, to Donut Press and Arts Council England for a Mentoring Award in 2009, to Faber and Faber/Arts Council England for a Faber New Poets Award in 2009, and to the Arts Council England for a Grants for the Arts Award in 2011.

Thanks and love also to Ed Atkins, Emily Berry, Mark Ford, Annie Freud, John Stammers, and to Jake Moulson and my family for all that's in the book and all that's not in the book.

CONTENTS

At First, the Only Concern Is Milk, More or Less

The baby had been guaranteed to reach us and came
with hair and no clothes. It's not surprising,
given the expedition. HellO, we said.

The task is to think things up. We said words like:
Ha, what's not a strange place? and In the field, look!
the calf's commitment to a routine dairy surge.

This is how it would be if it were possible to forget
Europe and sweat-shopped salopettes
and the smell of horses' noses and that the sky
is an identikit and words are identikits.

A dense love is under construction. There is more to say
and less is said – least of all Mother, I can't bear to
outlive you, which is all, really, that matters.
Sooner or later, it is actual trousers.

But where's the baby that's going to be
conned one second by the words, think them relevant?
The nurses retreated to a disinfected lobby.
What else? She was a whole person, but small.

Hello from This Position

Ladies and Gentleman, the lights
are off in an extravaganza of expectation.
Yes it is enlightening, high
in the dark, waiting to fly by the toes,
wearing a few decorative flourishes.
I am an unstuck cerise sequin, dangled
from the sky's last thread.
Your upturned faces are a ripple
in a pink-ish blanket.
But an upside-down person
is just an upright person
inverted. Night-time is just daytime
with canvas over it.
It will all be trash when the show's over.
And what is the big old world
but one big old tent.

A Dramatic Look inside the Heart Makes for Interesting Viewing

'Life is too contemporary,' says the heart.
'It's a nouvelle gymnasium with fountains of waste paper.' Or:

'Hi!' And: 'I'd like to make a discovery!'
These are just examples.

From the bar off the lobby, where peanuts are always freshest,
comes the sound of chewing. My heart could tell you:

'I spent an hour on the cross-trainer.'
It could tell you: 'This worked off the day's fat

tensions with a whiplash quality. Then I went for a sauna,
if there is a sauna.' Ease of communication

has ruined the heart's eloquence, for the moment.
As for me, I live by moving. All that's modern has movement.

I keep promising myself, one of these days
we'll exist underwater. My heart could tell you:

'People are dwarfed by the heart, alive in its real-time subplot.
I paddled through some lesser-known banlieues

of the deep end, to give it further thought,
the whole shapeless narrative of my untravelling.'

Heliocentric Cosmology

Got what?
asked my husband through a mouthful of mashed potato.
I was at home with my husband, eating mashed potato.

Two miniscule but unequal balls of mashed potato
dropped from his mouth onto the mashed potato.
It was like when Galileo dropped balls of the same material

but different masses from the Leaning Tower of Pisa,
except Galileo didn't use his mouth or mashed potato,
and the ground isn't a plate of mashed potato.

I've got it!
My husband looked up from the mashed potato.
I've got it!

I slammed my fist into the central, glowing platter of mashed potato.
It was hot, for mashed potato.
Orbs leapt.

They were loose crumbs of unmashed potato.
Some moved towards the mashed potato.
Some moved away from the mashed potato.

I had discovered that the earth goes around the sun.
Copernicus pre-discovered it.

Rumination on 25mm of Cotton

It's the hammerless C-string of the world's stupid piano.
Between my left and right hand, above the covers

whipped up like the Urals, it's the rope over an abyss.
It's a travesty of hand-stitching, a decapitation.

Whose cotton limb? It dangles from my thumb
and forefinger. The universe slackens in its shadow.

Sir, Herr, Monsieur, Dottore, M'Lord,
Your Honour – I tore it from its felted home

in palsy-walsy boredom. The long sound of the wind /
the hypnotic high-pitch / a rhapsody from the alley.

Or it was the spoutings of small whales on asphalt
carried via mothballs in the wardrobe.

For a moment, the thread was immense. I plucked it. Hard.
Mute hint of our bond with fluff, it hangs in night's unbound girdle.

Where and when will the barriers be in operation?

If not, why not use fingers to hold back
the swelling orgasm of wallpaper?
In the corridor at last, is that an armband or
a skin infection? Which plant would you be
and if the body is a great creation why wait
indoors with it? What matters most? Are you
this woman? How would you/she sing
under physical pressure? Why not? What
are the barriers and do they smell
of wood-smoke or human inventions
like keyhole surgery, the cold of refrigeration?

An Alternative to Television

I kept my hands busy in the park,
emphasising cuticles with a 4B pencil.

There is no why, I told the gardener
when he passed on his ride-on mower.

There was though – endorphins from shaven grass,
slashed at the height of its lawlessness,

as I would explain to myself afterwards,
going at the fingernails with a putty rubber.

The gardener didn't hear.
Not far from his rotating blades,

I was an ant with its back to the sky.
He was high on it too, his moulded seat

or the true size of the universe,
or whatever it was in my nostrils beneath

my eyes through which
one moment it's day the next it's not day.

Within the Cooling-off Period

Anti-essential days, a Thinker called them.
You might know we were in the new half
of the twenty-first century, enlarging
a pixel here or there without bursting anything.
SELENE Spacecraft had just blazed into the atmos.
3D goggles were en route to common usage.
My niece (not yet conceived), threw her huge
full-colour romper suit against the textured walls
of my imagination. It was like this: from a drop of water,
a logician could infer the Atlantic Ocean.

'Check it out!' – this was how people spoke –
'Your safety is in danger!' Visiting firemen
inspected our spoiled electric blankets with faces
with the look of faces about to be forgotten.
Safety, they implied, grows scarcer every second.
'Waskikkin, Firefighters? Multi-way plugs
in the overloaded bit wait for you
to bend and disconnect them.' Chockfull'o-know-how,
a fireman's arm in three dimensions
helped to make the present coherent.

Until then-then SELENE space-icles! Off
into lunar landscape to be a god, ciao-ciao!
A selection of feelings was contagious.
Via the National Grid, we shared experiences,
but we were alone at the sockets.
'Salvage me, Cookie!' – this aimed at the fireman –
'You, me, here in the riotous electrical pumping
of English winter. No. Hold it. *Ich habe* left a tap running.'
I can't go into the meaning of all this, except to say
it was not clear if we were naked or pretending.

Relational Epistemology

'It's whatever you want it to be,' said my father
after he bisected My Little Pony and used her in a sculpture.
At bedtime he read me Kafka's short fiction.

'All men are not idiots,' my mother advised,
'but beware of Structuralists;
life will never be a matter of signifiers and signs.'

She gave up her copy of *Someday My Prince Won't Come*
with a dedication: 'Darling, Don't be limited
by propositional modes of representation! xx'

Preparation of Rich Cherry Genoa was methodological.
My father paraphrased Merleau-Ponty: '*The toucher touching touched.*'
His hands around the mixing bowl, she sifted sugar.

It helped them contextualise the relationship between Self
and Other. Phenomenology at the dinner table was not unusual.
My brother queried so-called 'pepper', so-called 'ketchup',

ingested as if objective fact. The colour 'red' is not universal.
Mainly, my sister slept at any hour.
'See!' said my mother,

'The claim that all experience might be mediated by language
is one all women know to be preposterous.
And besides, Wittgenstein is dead.'

Over dessert, however, she absolved him
on account of her cake and his raisins. 'It's like Ludwig said,
raisins may be the best part of a cake

but a bag of raisins is not better than a cake.
My cake isn't, as it were, thinned-out raisins,
as you will know from experience.'

Ablutions

The bathtub makes me weak –
my heartbeat under water.
Salts, oils, sodium laureth sulphate:
I am a mountain in a lake.
From the corridor, *The Romantic Sounds of Xavier Cugat*;
I synchronise my loofah.
My big toe turns the hot tap.
Oh God, the changing temperature of bathwater!
Hot and cold I understand;
tepid means less than ever.
How hard it is to get things right.
How devastating you looked today across Soho Square
in your pink cashmere sweater,
your man-bag over your left shoulder.
Like soap I am loquacious
and I give myself up trying to say it.
Who was it that first thought of washing?
Your eyes are blue, I have loved you
since I noted your lashes in profile.
I didn't do it deliberately –
I was distracted
the way foam is distracted from water
and clings all over my contours.

What We Learn from Fantasy

– Belief in the tabletop
napkin dispensers that get our chins clean
as we pull the moment to tatters

and cry that there is no difference
between a face and a luxury item.

Both are in excess of thought
which is not the brain's function which is action!
Sure, the mind is not Raskolnikov napping,

though it is hungry and handsome.
Almost nothing corresponds to what goes on

in its sprung-floor playground except certainty
that days spew out like headlines
through a web-press as big as a building.

THEN A MAN IN A GORILLA SUIT HELD ME;
it was ~~like~~ deliverance.

Invention, it transpires, is contactless love-making.
It is the saucy dream of toothpaste hauliers
and the validity of oral hygiene. It is safe sex,

in some trendy poses, with the possibility
of more gallant kinds of cheesecakes.

In Tokyo, in the year 2003,
I overheard, the ground rolled continuously. Say,
who among us doesn't care to picture

the architectonic platelets that chafe below
the surfaces on which all people are shaken.

Devoted, Hopelessly

The only men it's safe for me to love are dead –
O'Hara, Stevens, Berryman. They send me to my desk,
or down the road to get black grapes, fit, and ideas.

Simon's hair was black and untameable.
Tuesdays, I stop at the library for poetry.
Hair's all very well; ideas take commitment.

At twenty-eight Charlotte Brontë feared herself a spinster.
Married soon after; died in pregnancy. I make marginalia:
'women are getting older all the time', etcetera.

In snow outside my window, Sam wrote 'Marry me!'
Days pass in gestures. I didn't hold his hand tightly.
He left me a message: 'We all need to be editors.'

I read the Index of First Lines aloud,
tell myself 'I need to be alone to be more',
meet Ben, by chance, by the derelict jobcentre.

He tells me: 'There's a lot of bad love going around.'
On the concrete, a snail is a comma
or an apostrophe, depending on context.

Le Parc

Every fifth Tuesday of the month my grandfather would meet with Monsieur Duchamp in le jardin public. Et voilà! Marcel digressed by the weeping beech tree. The hanging branches touched the ground. Being an artist, he said in squeezed English as he probed the foliage, is like crawling on your hands and knees along a narrow tunnel just to wash your filthy hands in the sink at the end of it, and then spending the rest of your life trying to get out backwards. A nut in a husk hit the soil. At any time though, my grandfather observed, you might be hauled out by the ankles.

Dear Johnny Bunny,
J. Bubs,
Hello ducks,
Dear Original Californian Sun-Dried Raisins,

Dear John Baldessari.

This is a surprise. You know, the way the inside of your mouth feels
when you gargle alcohol or accidentally get a mouthful of the ocean.
Huh.

What I'm trying to say is: when I close my eyes, all I see is a
six-foot-seven figure of Man. (Your white beard.) I have done for a
long time, ever since I first saw a face without a nose. That was your
quoi fraiche of the noughties.

We were leaving by slow bus, moving past a noseless Grecian statue
(NOT the Venus de Milo). Remplir une fiche it said to the right of
the Kestner Gesellschaft advertisement. On a dotted line, I pencilled
'mes cheveux'. Tirez pas mes cheveux, my lover said. Oui, d'accord,
I replied. There was candyfloss on the breeze. I have the idea that
something MIGHT happen, he said, but not necessarily. (There was
froth on his upper lip.)

Back then it felt like things were getting taken apart. Now it feels like
they're being put together. Is this you? Or me?

What's with(out) all the noses? It would never have occurred to me,
the noses. And I think about stuff like this all the time. What to take
out when packing my baggage. I just spent twenty minutes trying to
think of another facial feature that would work as well *in absentia*.
I got nothin'.

It was lonely with the poster of the woman with no nose and the
man with no eyes. When we left the Czech Republic, the lover said
Could we stop horsing around for ten minutes. PLEASE.

At the autobusové nádraží, everyone was French kissing like an advert for sexy deodorant.

I don't know why I have to tell you this today. On the other hand, I'm not going to write a whole letter and then throw it away. No, sir. One doesn't learn about social intercourse by thinking about it. Although — I must confess — I accidentally tore a photograph of my lover's face in half once and lost half to the wind, which has left an overspill of guilt. I don't want to be a litterbug! Here's a thought, John-o: Maybe you could tell me about a way of ripping that works with one hand and leaves the other free to steer the bicycle.

I suppose you're just back from 'going to the studio for the day' with the pinking shears tucked into your left back pocket. Is the day hospitable, and light, with pick-up trucks advancing like whopping great fatsos, etcetera? There they all go, gyrating across the San Andreas Fault.

Despite everything, I am determined to get to the point. We always want to be looking. To find out. If you're calculating my follicles, I can tell you: one-plus-one-plus-one-plus-equals-. Schuyler said Giorgione said that's what painting can do, show everything at a glance. Cut Horizontal or Vertical? Cut here or CUT there? How many?
Cut!
I expect you're wondering whether I've read the entire volume of Ulysses beside my bed. It's important to try and figure out what the difference is between a part and a whole. A part can become a whole and a whole can become a part and, really, I don't see why I wasn't born John Baldessari instead of

Let me conclude by reiterating the main point.

We must meet sometime for a chatette in Frisco; or perhaps in wetlands in the Lea Valley. Enjoy your western wafts of coolth, thwacking in off the broad Pacific. It's not possible to describe the climate here. We lie low like coy carp.

German Phenomenology Makes Me Want to Strip
and Run through North London

Page seven – I've had enough of *Being and Time*
and of clothing. Many streakers seek quieter locations
and Marlborough Road's unreasonably quiet tonight.
If it were winter I'd be intellectual, but it's Tuesday
and I'd rather be outside, naked, than learned –
rather lap the tarmac escarpment of Archway Roundabout
wearing only a rucksack. It might come in useful.
I can't take any more of Heidegger's *Dasein*-diction,
I say as I jettison my slippers.

When I speak of my ambition
it is not to be a Doctor of Letters
or to marry Friedrich Nietzsche, it turns out,
or to think better.
It is to give up this fashion for dressing.
It is to drop my robe on the communal stairs
and open the front door onto the commuter hour,
my neighbour, his Labrador, and say nothing
of what I know or do not know, except what my body announces.

Darling, You Missed a Revelation

Jerry Appis said, a dead horse, that's what it needs,
the outdoor pool on the day of Sam Smith's funeral.
Don't you think he looks *reassuring*, our Mr Wilberforce,
the handsome beast, smooth and buttery,
his twisted hammerhead, his tongue rubbery?

At the funeral/pool-party everyone nodded.
Jerry Appis was known for his ideas to overcome bereavement.
Mrs Smith's eyes were glossy like *peau de soie*
and her whole face whiter than bathroom sealant
in her mountainous excitement.
'How la-di-da! How *eques*trian!'
Aesthetics and death could be reconciled.

Everyone has pool parties, it's what Sam would have wanted.
Sam loved Americana before the electrocardiogram.
He was forced to draw up a diagram of the hole
he'd leave behind – a whole hole or half a hole /
who would dig it and pour him into it.

Jerry Appis chased a girl, gave a little talk on love,
how its shape inspires our confectionery,
how it feels like a squashed grape
carried in a pocket, or something too large to curl up in a ball
and throw away – like a rural landscape or a suitcase.
Nothing in this world was made for him
unless it came vulcanized at 69° Celsius.

Hell! cried Jerry, show me a pool
that's not improved by a sunken horse
and I'll show you laughter resmbling lukewarm tears,
moved at the stale theme of disbelief. Only those
who still have hope can capitalise on sobbing.

1960s Monochrome Hollywood Paraphernalia ($47, collection only)

• **1 sizeable hoard** of defunct birds (some deader than others). Includes an owl (unusually rigid) and anything else you would want to see in flight in spring (mounted, in a parlour). All come with tiny bones crunched into a museum of artistic poses (if you lean in you can hear viscera or sky curdle steeply). In addition, a period of hurley-burley just beginning. Anticipation that roughly hovers overhead like an arched eyebrow or a buzzard before supper. A kind of rigorous love. Also: shadows (what they are and what goes on in them). Darkness, generally. (A lot of clouds bumping around the periphery.) Undertones. Overtones. Violin strings (lightly scratched) in upper registers. Blanched hair of a certain period. Tiny gloss eyes pinned in the middle distance. Miscellaneous beaks and a man's mouth, all in nipping distance. 1 devilishly wet December to accompany a tight-fitting office, unlikely to change (unless papers get shuffled). Plus: Pale-faced loon from motel foyer (comes with upturned collar, undernourished, bearing sandwiches). Could I…uh…do you…uh…here's the…uh… (classic examples of awkward speech patterns). 1 little-frequented plot of mud. 1 woman's voice (disembodied). Sturdy rain (trying to prove something). My trusty umbrella.

National Geographic's Indian Subcontinent Photo Gallery
Where All of Life Is in Appearances, and Just outside of Them

How long, Editor, until my face resembles the bonnet macaque
as the bonnet macaque resembles Samuel Beckett?
Somewhere, everywhere, monkeys show signs of wear.
I should rather be pretty, but I don't, so there.

SPEECH TO BE DELIVERED AT THE FIRST CONVENIENT OCCASION

"Why be afraid of speaking
when you have something to say
cherish it as a one-handed pianist
cherishes his one hand of fingers.
            You see it's not that the world is devoid of ideas
                        but that ideas are usually wrong.
                                    Stop thinking about them.
            When you want to know the news
take off your trousers
think of Nothing. Imagine
Nothing has come upon you unawares
            at the self-service checkouts.
                        Study its face like you are in love
                        with an exotic but normal huge metal archway.
            What utensils do we need to eat The Future?
Let's let things glue become puffy.
Remember when I was this tall
a flourishing know-nothing at the height
            of her drawing pencils!
                        Is this true why did I say it?
                        No I tell you you mustn't believe anything.
                        Stay irresponsible say what you imagine.
            Choose meat in everything but flesh!
Who butchered the sausages?
It's more difficult than people think
to make ideas simple. Ideas
            are like boiled sweets lodged in the throat for hoiking
                        a hand on your shoulder
                        the primary experience of bathing, and –

Go nuts! The sea shouldn't be deprived
of naked bodies in this weather.
Though we're not about to discover Australasia
                    we can travel with purpose
                         using the best inventions of others
                              like Danish public transport.
Don't summarise the idea in one easy sentence:
I never thought I'd win so I haven't prepared much."

Red Slugs in Every Irrelevant Direction

You will be surprised by your red-headed children,
a yogi had foretold in Calcutta for baksheesh. And I was surprised.
Where had they come from and where were they going?

If, at that moment, I had held my breath
and waited for the sky to get a move on,
it wouldn't have made any difference to their progress.

They wanted to be everywhere, damn their chunky souls.
Wait, Mummy – let me in! They slunk up to the back door.
The clouds had given them permission

to secrete their protective mucus across surfaces.
As IF I was going to fall for this garbage –
my red-headed children, imagine.

Up close, the grass must sound like hundreds of blunt razors.
Good job you've got your tough skin from your father
(whoever *he* was), I thought, but didn't say

as the minty squall inside our troposphere
pelted the put-upon buds and leaves
and their thoughtless heads, if slugs have heads.

The Horsey Mail

I send this to you by overnight horse.
He whips east like the 277.
In bed I stare at a ceiling
and see you yesterday, from the top deck
of a bus, cycle over the junction.
You wobbled moderately
(was it the wind or loose-chippings or me?),
with your legs – I thought I saw – shaved
for aerodynamics. And anyway,
everything and nothing rides on him,
and the road surfaces are uneven
and his forelocks are wavy and so is your hair
when it's longer and that makes me lonely
so give him oats and blackcurrant jam
and damn the vitamin tablet in my throat
that keeps me awake, it's not the morning
without you. And forgive him –
he may have nothing to give when he gets there.

An Encounter in the New Language

In the washing machine's drum is an odd regatta.
Many days turn into a knot of coloured hosiery
at the STOP of a rapid spin cycle.

Bookcases aren't reassuring, love.
Literature is too exciting, enmeshes you in its concerns
and irregular verbs, half-lost in personal sundry items.

Disengagement from this scene could take some time.
Tights don't help, have no authority, say nothing aloud.
All in all, tights have it easy.

They're a mashed-up corporation of legs and feet,
indifferent to global events and individual responsibility,
like seven proud daughters in an epic of coincidences

exhilarated from a whirl around the great lake,
not happy because their toes are soaked, not unhappy
because their toes are soaked.

Although You Do Not Know Me, My Name Is Patricia

For the record, we are undertaking research into Love, or Something Similar Assembled in the Factories of Imagination.

Claire, my assistant, is sorry she couldn't be here, by the way. I, too, am sorry she couldn't fit through your bathroom window, even when naked. 'Now pass me back my knicks and cash and let me go refine my statistics!' Beneath streetlights, her sweat glands recalled the margarine in my carrier bag. Having lubricated my surfaces, I slithered through the chink, alighting on your cabinet.

From the array of dyspepsia remedies, I deduce that you are a communist pedagogue and your wife an apprentice bohemian. Although Flossie was never exactly a cabaret dancer, she demanded to be called Flossie and was in a panic to marry. Panic and relentless love are easily mistaken.

We make up for it by making things up, spilling our adventures to anyone who'll listen. Some share life, like two unequal halves of a Chelsea Bun, with a stranger. Some release the sugared non-half into the mouth of a stranger. Some realise the unequal-half-fiddle once the sugar's all swallowed by a mouth that won't be around forever. The Factories' inventions may be the high-spot along the damp bricks of years, Claire would deduce, if Claire could be here,

Claire would say your miniature soap collection belies a marriage of sex and pecuniary convenience. Tons of sex. Twice a night for a month, then every other night for two months. Soon it was three times a week for a year, then once a week. Now, almost never. Don't worry though, the future is broken anyway. Something went wrong a while back. Why else would we huddle together in cities, if not to feel better (if not safe exactly).

You're an Architect and I Want to Make Dinner for You

Just as I slice the treacle tart you halt my hand,
ask me to regard its lattice. You elaborate with permanent ink,
kitchen paper – your ideas sink through to the table. Steadily,
evening arrives from the East.

My bedsit is modest, my world is changing – seated
opposite you and your 0.2 fineliner, it includes all possible
universes. The pastry is homemade. We dream in multiple dimensions –
lines are trellises, extensions, non-Euclidean geometries –
see, you say, how the shortcrust lets us see beyond it! Yes,
our windows will be curvilinear. I pour the cream,
neatly fold your drawing (twice), nearly forget to eat.

The One Coat that Could Have Made Winter Worth Living through

Danielese, Danielese, my coat's been stolen
from the heap of party outerwear in your sitting room.
If I drove the world's crammed bus, I'd brake and loot
its side-pockets. A person has my coat,
along with the filthy history of streets we trod,
my railcard and guarantee of sophistication.
My personality will never be as pure-new-woollen.
We must hunt for my coat, Danielese, everywhere between
the front door and the art students at full-throat
in your kitchenette, thrust in flat-pack cubbyholes.

No more ample cuffs. No more superior liaisons
with coat-hooks. I don't ask much of life, except to scrape
meaning out of the possessions that possess us.
So you understand, Danielese, it isn't vanity;
every year it'll be the coldest day of the year again.
In the meantime, there'll be weeks of coatlessness
and of waiting for my hair to grow – a prolonged substitute
for the immediacy of buttons.

So long, Danielese. And thanks for the low lighting.
At least you can be sure that I won't forget
the fiddle-player who played on until god knows when
beside the dim arena beside the punchbowl, and the punchbowl
beside the coat-pile, and the coat-pile, piled high with coats.

Nudity of Cattle

They look as if they understand what it's like to pull on a swimsuit.
'We give it less thought.' / 'None at all, on occasion.'
Their look has withstood generations.

Meanwhile, over in the local baths,
there goes Katerina in too-wet water.
It comes at her in bursts of shallowness and depth.

She dreams of imitating these Lorettas, Karlottas, Claudettas,
Florindas, Astrids, Marquishas and Elaines
with their jumperless self-possession.

Meanwhile, backstrokers advance in limp postures.
She has tried to beat them, god knows she has tried, sometimes
at a violent level something like warfare.

Bodies accentuated by swimsuits have secrets, secrets.
Past the No Petting sign, long hair moults in thin bundles.
The bare facts will arrive between here and the changing room.

Meanwhile, thank god for the cows, face-to-face with each other
and terrifying existence, who reveal that there is nothing to hide
except what we keep hidden, mostly.

The Distance between England and America

Much could begin like this: a large man,
tie slackened, voice buoyed up by altitude.
My mind's elsewhere –
the air-conditioning. It's cold.
Above the Atlantic he bellows long vowels to me,
and I'm cabined, window-seated, polite.
With my English tone, I'm inadvertently provocative –
No more salted pretzels for me, thanks Jeff.

At the sound of Charles Darwin's bassoon,
earthworms, apparently, writhed.
Jeff booms: Pittsburgh, golf clubs, his search for a wife.
I twist in my seat – suggest something,
in my movement, of all evolution.
His blanket folds back like an invitation
to navy shadows and polyester.
Heat and anything could happen under there.

Oh, take your loafers off, Jeff –
throw them in the aisle.
Your gusto can conquer my boredom, our bed can be the sky.
It's warming up. We won't be sleeping.
For almost nine hours beneath United Airlines covers
we'll share everything but thought.
In the morning, white bread rolls and Columbus, Ohio.
Women distribute plastic cutlery in the night.

Fingers Are Not Ignorable

You collect filth as gophers stockpile alfalfa.
Bunch of average nobodies, everything unduly concerns you.

Run on, my flock, into the hacked-up semi-weather!
Pull on your fingerless uniforms, semi-incognito.

Of course, you are loose-toothed amnesiacs, chomping
into the whole waxy ball, chattering. You are minor injuries,

children, every one pinching and falling. Take hold
of the bomber jacket, unzip its zipped-up zipper. It's your duty

to be attentive. Or you are more similar to lovers,
unknowable to onlookers, thingamajigs heated up

in armpits! Remember the mind has uncharted districts.
Fork up events. Prime them to happen.

Rhythmically julienne the carrots. I will stab a kitchen knife
between you to keep you almost co-operative.

Unapproachable Regions

Evening catches.
I work out fourth position against the banister,

articulate who I need to be.
Music makes me crumple and rain is likely tomorrow.

By the attic window, the amaryllis.
I press the fingerboard, practise.

In the hills, I was glad and weak at the top.
What I cannot express, the violin cannot help with.

Actually, I'm Simply Trying to Find My Dressing Gown Sash

Matter can't vanish. But, having checked my waist
(coffee percolator, compost heap, plug hole, deep freeze, U-bend,
consulted the moth with a philosopher's expression on the door mat
(dead)), what's left in this place to frisk or rely on.

Best to walk off in a straight line towards a recollection
of the bird feeder or to answer the daily telephone call
where someone called Cyril calls me
someone called Jennifer. There has been an omission.

Unlike my belt, Cyril would never leave Jennifer unsupported.
That's crud, he'd declare ('crud', a word he loathes
until it makes him joyful) and surprise her with a ribbon.
The sides of Jennifer's dressing gown would not flap inevitably.

Who? I say, or Oh, yes, or, Forget her, Cyril, we live for encounters
ahead of us, there's only so much breath. Only runners
should be up at this hour, running for their lives.
And Mo and Billy, of course, who will call Jennifer any minute

from their farmhouse kitchen. Then it's Suzy (your niece, aunty Jennifer),
calling me (Jennifer) on her tea break, by which time the logic
of logic has been disconnected, and where am I, reflecting
parenthetically on wrong numbers and over-connectedness

in my under-connected dressing gown that billows
during morning duties while Mo and Billy kiss each other passionately
and Suzy wishes Jennifer happy birthday
and all I want is a bathrobe with a belt attached to it.

The gown sags in its absence while I upend then dig around
the bin bag, looking for a truth too obvious
to recognise in the used plastics, dammit, and all along,
up to the elbows, doubtful of its existence.

Jesus Christ

He called by to ask questions: 'Did you ever thump a nose? Maybe an informal whack, fourteen years ago? To dry-run the bleeding?'

I wanted this man on my side. He had access to)**£!..?^%! . He seemed no more than the apron of a face, a way of looking.

You could say he had the veneer of a ladies' man in the smash-up of his career. A man, or a desolate landscape. A trampled-on forest. Yet still, strangely attractive. Death overwhelms even mediocrity.

Why must it always end this way? 'The face is the only avant-garde we have,' I replied. 'And the name. A good name is promotable.'

**The Baby [hereafter referred to as 'The Baby'] hereby contracts
with The Mother [hereafter referred to as 'The Mother'] –**

to make it difficult to see how this daytime interior
got by before the arrival of her wet-look coiffure.
It collapses your synapses, the likeness
to the armchair's tugged corners.

The Mother is up and moving laterally, making
assumptions about not-to-be-missed ear infections,
careful not to knock into sterilised bottles.
Minor details swell while the plump energy bounces.

To compensate, names will be designated to Everything
as if Everything is under control.
Time will be diced into a number of segments. Now
it is one thousand four hundred and forty minutes per day.

The Baby will look peppier every second,
reminding The Mother of mutual human frailty,
that names are indecent, that there is a 57% chance
there's more to life than the best Pierre Bonnard paintings,

a small chance of fog of the kind that flourishes
in Ferrara and munches the region away.
The Baby will sleep on her back. The Mother
will have lived through other, less costly, more badly-lit, times.

(I could mention when I was a baby, when
the price of doughnuts was lesser, when
bees were pleased, when milk was Champagne, when
I didn't know the difference between myself and the table leg, when)

The Baby's tossed coverlet is her signature.
Standing before a pair of The Mother's
outstretched hands on a floor propped up
by gravity, there will be no going back.

The Baby will get used to it, sadly: purple earmuffs,
rhinoplasty, ritual polygamy, Recommended Retail Prices, art
with a capital R, Mah-Jong, instant upload, *a priori* knowledge,
'humane' mousetraps, the off-side rule, (scheißehaus!), electrolysis,

joyeux noel, grrr, apricot-dusting, sexist puppet shows,
the mind's thin orgy, politician-bashing+peachaberry cobbler.
Both parties, by mutual agreement, will hold hands in mittens
as if spooning in, possibly, long-johns, one of them notionally wiser,

while The Baby doesn't wonder when
The Mother will stop thinking of her, The Baby, as The Baby.

Some Kind of Memento Mori

Oh yes, the woolly mammoths are all gone.
For twenty three and a half hours a day I forget
and then a 40-watt bulb blows as I turn it on.
It's something unspoken, the burnt-out bayonet –
its filament no longer incandescent,
the electric current without an outlet, and I see –
not much has changed since the Pleistocene.
Removal of the bulb is a change of epoch.
These days, there are elephants in Africa, elephants
in India, the new gloom of silhouettes and table lamps,
new pearl bayonets in my cupboard in their boxes.
But the woolly mammoths are gone even in Siberia.
The glass bulb is spent, though shapely in its socket.
I've changed plenty of bulbs but this one's gone
and brought to light the shadows that go on in shadows
or, as I think of it, yes, woolly mammoths.

Digression on the Col d'Aubisque

I could say a lot about a lot of thinking, but my heart
knocks at the bends, or at you in profile,
and I'd rather hear the stereo. We're right on the edge
of the gravel and of knowing each other,
driving, familiarity, the line
between intimacy and dying.
Our breath's on the windscreen.
I've left my shoes in the boot.

I want to call out to the horses in the mist:
I've known so much about insignificant themes.
I've known nothing. Not like the way a horse
knows grass. I count all the men I've ever kissed.
But I'm with you, almost over the verge
and, if we slid off now, the privilege would be mine –
not to know if it was the beginning,
or the end, or your fault for steering or mine
for, say, at that moment reclining my seat.

I'd know my red toenails
against your walnut-trim dashboard
and shout to the horses:
'It wasn't the hairpin bends; it was something else!'
I'd know you in ways
they can't understand: high up, brief.
Let me change gear while you drink pear juice.
Beyond your bonnet is the rest of the world.
Mountains – I can barely see them.

Birds in Inflexible Bird Bodies

Here would be ideal
to get stuffing the avian backlog.
It's as though an owl had let himself in
and said, Now, a nice dark place like this,
if I really put my back into it, I can give up
my free-blowing birdlife to stand impaled
and unfolded like an antique love letter
yanked from a dirty drawer.
It's almost certain that, inside
his iron head, he thinks it over.
Or it's as though a woodpigeon dropped by
to wait for the dénouement and waited
long after the wait had finished.
If these birds could think or plan,
they too would wonder what
keeps their heads attached, who
sewed up the identical side-seams, why
the little nylon threads that hold
everything together don't just snap.

You might say we've got it all. Get a load of the lighting.

Come right in. Find a chair. Make yourself at home.

If I'm not mistaken, you're already in the room,
already seated.

Where?

You're here to avoid situations. Rooms are full
of situations – the Utopian values of Esperanto, the
possibilities of a shared International Style, people.

We get lost by looking. Here is where the wall was,
the innuendo of curtains.

Inevitable furniture has slipped in, along with a sense
of failed promise, the conversations I could never have
with my grandmother. She thought chairs were largely
demeaning and moronic.

Oh. Is he dead?

Knee-high booties are indecorous, foot-to-face with his rabbit-like body
before the bin men have eradicated our rubbish. Dead rabbit,
you make me a tactless stroller with my hands in my pockets, whistling.

Reality rumbles by with four fatal wheels.
Excuse the rabbit and all vegetation he offended. Touching the dead
marries them to us, us too death marries. White sheep with brown faces
are a reassurance at this time, as is a shower-proof jacket.

Your mucky side against my mucky side, dear rabbit, dead rabbit –
how similar to ours your years in random warrens, rabbiting
with your rabbit pals, going along your rabbity ways out of habit!

Judder Our Bones like a Dadaist Manifesto

Let's not go over the top
of the universe, eating pieces of cloud,
destined to become space statistics.

We don't see much placed in a pinhole'd box
with stingy parameters, administered to by Schmidt-Haberkamp,
shiny as a German teaspoon in a hotel breakfast room –

'Yes, Madam?' –
who speaks so well it's spoken badly, who makes
air travel attractive by skilful packaging.

How about a mint julep, since the interior is…de*press*ing,
like all store cupboards. Thank you for the strip-lit dark
and pressure-sealed exit. Would you save my tiny life

if the guttering and choking meant what it sounds like?
Das ist eine kleine nachtmuzik, it's the g-force to our holdall.

What difference does it make and how are we supposed to
see where we are / get our bearings.
How do trolley staff manage to gel hair so short?

Gel can be used as a verb in that context.
Schmidt-Haberkamp laughs but it's not a real laugh, nothing is
destroyed by it. Only our nostrils

will be defeated in the interim
by the lack of all smells except tax-free perfume, and our wits
if we *really* think about tea at this altitude

or of putting our watches forward to exist in the same time-zone
in which Ludwig van Beethoven existed.

James Grieve, One

I saw your apple before I saw your face.
Golden-cheeked, it glided in above a scarf
of the kind worn by men who play chess.
And marvellous how you could make it last
strategically, it seemed, by eating less
and talking more, as though each bit that passed
your lips were a course in some slow repast;
your restraint! I was part-starved, stapled to my place.

My Braeburn I bite at eight o'clock; you lovely thing,
you made me do it. The window suspends
the creases of the evening sky, my clothes fold to the floor
like hot towels. Vivid as the crimson curtains, I sing
canticles from the second storey as if all flesh depends
on the sinking of teeth through air: premise of our rapport.

When the City Centre's at a Standstill, It's Really Quite a Thrill to Lie in the Road and Read Herman Melville

When the high street is a blackened toenail
at my foot's stub-end, more bruised and less alive,
where's the growling sea? The sky filled with harpoons?

Herman Melville is Herman Melville.
Herman Melville is like being in love, unsustainably.
You have to scram to the gutter, cling to Herman Melville.

Herman Melville.
Will my last, solitude-loving synapse be pumiced by loiterers?
Is there no law against junk thought? Is this modernity?

Is the only solution an unarmed cell, a sky-scraping mountain,
a single unfinishable book, no view, a revolution
involving the totally unconsumable, Herman Melville?

Bogentechnik

1

We see a lot of that here. Morning.
For the last forty-nine, I have worked on chin position.
Wrist angle is a kind of retribution.
Next, the scary leap to highest D-sharp,
the abandonment of philosophy.

2

Forgive me for playing to you impromptu fashion,
standing up. It seems indecent to sit at a table
with my arms at these gradients.
'Your fingers are *too*   *too*
A virtuoso does not serve music; it serves her.' And so on.
'Hmmmmmmnnnnn?'
(Feedback so crushing I resort to a sea breeze with legwarmers.)

3

During the stay, there has arisen a hilly quality to living.
The hill. The Bowing Technique.
The Olympic-size bath taken daily with strangers.
(Human breakers and backwash. An underwater head.)

4

The lesson in fiddling starts again with redoubled dynamism.
'Miss. Yes, miss. No, miss. Jesus wept. And no wonder, by Christ.'
'It is humiliating having to present oneself
as an empty tube inflated by the mind.'

5

We waste time in the pool without wasting anything.
We reach a point where a single additional swimmer
makes a whole stack of swimmers.

It is hard to keep not-swallowing
the dead fly and chips of ear plug
having intercourse in our bathwater.

6

Violinless, I undergo a long weekend with baby vomit.
No match for it will be seen in millennia.
Like the lord's hands performing the Heimlich manoeuvre
on a barrel of yoghurt. Twiceover.

7

The drive back is not uneventful,
past the funfair in a single-decker.
The sky is black which, as you know, is the negation of colour.
Rosin the bow. Apply the full flatness. Tighten the hair.
Slacken the hair. Boil your water.
Instructions are a tourist's guide to basic phrases.

8

Leaving the county does not mark the end of The Doflein Method.
How to get a vibrato on an open G-string.
What to do. Fingering.
How to maximise the draft through
the Taiwanese candy-strings of my edible undies.

9

Adjust the pressure.
The boy up front has skin like a blanched almond,
the topography of a ladle-shaped profile.
His hand is in his trackie bottoms, cupping
I can only imagine.

Some Whales and Antonioni Died. This is What Happens. Some Men Wear Turtleneck Sweaters.

Then people were young
or they were not. Then the nearest woman
hoisted a Dachshund

from her rucksack. It was a time of hi-compression
thoughts which were no longer thoughts
of wide open spaces. You could say,

'I reached the vestibule of my wear and tear',
if vestibule is still a word. In London,
the sky did not take off. Then my eyes

became wetter before irregularly spaced images
in the cinema. The truth is there comes a time
when it is bodies that are fearful.

Humpback whales in Japanese seas
go unseen in obscene scenes. If there is no love
for animals, what are bodies telling us. What

should prevent a feat like that occurring – love
or a, perhaps, film where events are sequenced
as though they have a meaning.

The Horse Jacuzzi

hums in the corner, the only sound
on a quiet night. Water is pumped –
stable smells, the foamy purple tide.

Gush after gush trails her body curves
and, like a girdle or the most tender love,
clips her solid waist. She chafes and slams,

rubbing her legs, shanks, thighs –
flings her arrogant love-lock back,
her velvet helmet high.

Great big mountainous sports girl,
do you know that the stucco is peeling?
do you know that the heart will stop?

Steam's escaping. Observe: a freeze-frame
trickle of water, the distinct eyelashes,
the incessant weeping of drains.

If We Are in Favour of Motherhood, Let Us Not Be against the Great White Man-eating Shark

It has a conical snout.
It can go for weeks without meals.
When we flap our legs in its electromagnetic field,
let us remember that its teeth, as they come at us,
are just interested fingers, serrated.
It is given to no unseemly outcries.
It has no choice but to circle and circle to breathe.

And let us not forget that the Great White Man-eating Shark
brings forth its young alive.
On the whole, females are bigger than males.
They were mothers before humans were.
Indeed, it could be said that the Great White Man-eating Shark,
in a sense, *is* motherhood.
In a sense. It has a conical snout.
It simply wants to know: what kind of an object are you?
could you love me back?

How Things Haven't Changed

Through windows, the road is an extensive misunderstanding
confirmed by an engine. It is panoramic condensation.

On foot, it's a kerb, some raindrops,
two and half miles and so on until the art gallery,

Turkmenistan, the Russia-China border
where Przewalski's horses gallop for Ulan Bator. See ya!,

soles of my shoes, the puddles are on their way in.
Mongolian mares must be glad to be unshod, all-terrain.

A few more metres and my feet will be startled bathers
in cotton-rich outfits, high tide in the Barents Sea.

Help us, the cushioned insoles whine. Walk on! I order.
Fillies outdistance cobblers, bus stops, wetness.

It isn't possible to recall the first time I heard footfall
but it was as natural as small wild horses.

Goodbye. You can take this as my notice.

Plan C: become less obvious. It's been said I'm good with mammals.
More than that, I'm tremendous in a perceived crisis. I take control,
show spunk and affirmation.

For too long, I've been passing through one of those periods in
which significance is found only in dullness. I don't know what I
need. I need to get out of these wet leggings and into a dry Martini.

Let's prefer these pointless days while we can. Everything is linked.
Everything and nothing, to be accurate.

Heather Phillipson is an internationally exhibiting artist and award-winning poet. She received an Eric Gregory Award in 2008. Her pamphlet was published by Faber and Faber in 2009; her text *NOT AN ESSAY* by Penned in the Margins in 2012; and her first book-length collection, *Instant-flex 718*, by Bloodaxe Books in 2013.

As an artist, Heather Phillipson works with video, sculpture and live events. She has recently exhibited at venues including the Whitechapel Gallery (London), the ICA (London), BALTIC Centre for Contemporary Art (Gateshead), South London Gallery, Flat Time House (London), Zabludowicz Collection (London) and Kunsthalle Basel (Switzerland).